MAN'S BEST FRIEND

Introducing Wicked Willie in the title role

Cartoons by Gray Jolliffe

Text by Peter Mayle

Pan Books
London and Sydney

CONTD..:-

3

Foreword

There are almost as many names for a man's most intimate possession as there are for man himself.

Depending on the self-confidence of the owner, and the degree of esteem that exists between the two parties, these names vary from the optimistic (Big Steve, Oliver Twist) to the pessimistic (General Custer, The Sleeping Beauty); from formality (He Who Must Be Obeyed) to familiarity (Old Faithless); from Tom, Dick and Harry to Jean-Claude, Giorgio and Fritz.

The villain of this book is called Willie, a
handsome devil whichever way you look at him.

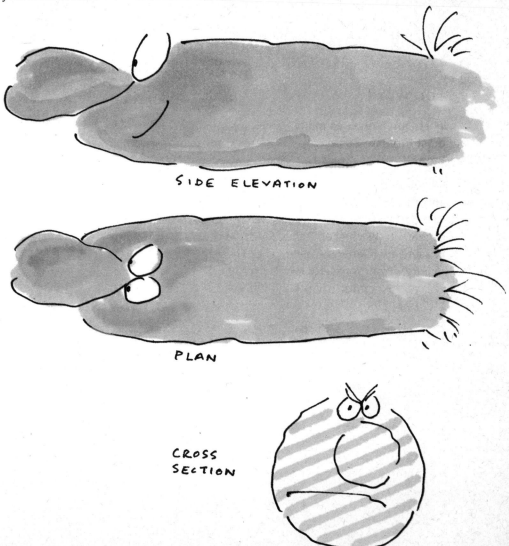

SIDE ELEVATION

PLAN

CROSS
SECTION

Behavioural patterns

A mainly nocturnal creature, spending daytime
(with some reluctance) beneath layers of
clothing. Will take every opportunity to escape
the confines of underpants in search of fun and
trouble. Has so far resisted all attempts at
domestication. Not to be trusted in pubs, the
Underground, lifts, on dance floors, or in the
cosmetic department of Harrods.

New light on the serpent theory

Ever since the dawn of creation, the serpent has been cast in the role of purveyor of magic apples and general mischief-maker. However, recent advances in scholarly research suggest a very different story. It started on a pleasant spring day in the Garden of Eden.

The seven ages
of man

Now that we know how all the trouble started, it comes as no surprise to find that man's entire lifespan is dominated, from a very early age, by what an eminent anthropologist calls *Dementia Guilielmi*, or the Willie Obsession. While precise timings will vary (particularly in Camden Town), most experts agree that the following stages of development can be identified.

As with Archimedes, the moment of revelation takes place in the bath. After several months of being entirely satisfied with his rubber duck, our baby looks down and – *Eureka*! – realizes that he has been born with a permanent toy attached to his person. Mothers who try to discourage this healthy interest should be warned that a frustrated infant could grow into an adult with rubber duck dependence, which can cause embarrassment and substantial psychiatrist's bills later in life.

What some people see as getting in a corner and talking dirty is, in fact, the first true sign of a sharing personality beginning to emerge. Why keep this treasure to yourself? It is the mark of a generous spirit to be frank and open in dealings with your peers, and at the same time a boy can learn the rudiments of peaceful negotiation: *'I'll show you mine if you show me yours'*. There's a lesson here for politicians. This kind of straightforward approach could put an end to the arms race.

Strange and wonderful reports are coming in from older boys. This is not only a purely functional object we have here, but potentially the source of untold pleasure. All is not yet clear to you, but you do know that something happens in the back seats of cars which is more fun than football. A driver's licence suddenly becomes essential. Girls become socially acceptable. Girls with cars and big back seats appear in your dreams. Your turn is coming up. And so is Willie.

Burning with zeal and ambition, your eye is firmly fixed on the managing director's job. Your friend, on the other hand, is much more interested in the managing director's secretary. Do not be misled by the career development survey which lists office politics as the main cause of executive failure. The real problem is the office party, which has claimed more victims than all the hatchet men of the West End and Threadneedle Street put together.

A time of grave peril, particularly for those single-minded men who have managed to avoid corporate entanglements so far. With years of blameless service behind you, the next step is Chairman of the Board, lunches with captains of industry, a profile in the *Financial Times*, and your very own executive loo. Alas, the beast below has other ideas. Inflamed by years of neglect, he leads you into a disastrous liaison with an exotic dancer at a sales conference and you are exiled to Central Filing in Basingstoke.

Your eyesight dims, and most of your other faculties lose their sharpness. But, with a selfish disregard for your heart murmur, the urge is still there. Your only hope is to follow this golden rule: never remove your trousers unless you are in the presence of a registered nurse, and even then insist on seeing her diploma. You can't be too careful these days.

Memory has now faded along with practically everything else, but occasional glimmers of recollection still occur. Strange to say, these are invariably pleasant – perhaps because it's comforting to find that some part of you is still intact, even though teeth and hair have long since gone.

Milestones in history

As in all lengthy struggles, each side has had its ups and downs, and it is illuminating to see how historical trends and sociological customs have led to the mess we're in today. The rot started shortly after woad became unfashionable.

The Dawn of Time

The invention of the loincloth represents a decisive victory for prehistoric Willie, who without this rudimentary form of shelter would have been too busy coping with frostbite and poison ivy to misbehave. In its early days, the loincloth as a source of warmth comes under fierce competitive pressure from fire, which is invented about the same time. The owner of the fire franchise eventually has to concede defeat after a series of painful experiments and badly singed customers. The loincloth wins, and thus the rag trade is born. (Note: no definitive proof is avilable to support the theory that designer loincloths once existed in Florida apart from some primitive cave drawings in the Men's Room of Miami Airport.)

The Dark Ages

Man strikes back. Hideous tales are circulated of the penalties which lie in store for those who indulge in fun and games – roasting in eternal flames, gibbering fits, hairy palms, withdrawal of credit facilities, etc. Everybody is dressed in sacks, except the armed forces, who are encased in steel trousers. High-born ladies are padlocked inside chastity belts, and an epidemic of rust rash spreads through the upper levels of society. It is these factors, and not the Black Death, which lead to an overall decline in world population.

The Renaissance

Again we see the insidious workings on the rag trade. Steel and sacking are out. Fine silks and gossamer are in. The Renaissance, a public relations scheme devised by an Italian designer in order to promote the codpiece, must be seen as a breakthrough period, supported by the statistical evidence of an upturn in population figures.

The Victorian Era

A valiant but flawed counterattack by man.
Objects of a lustful and inflammatory nature
such as female bottoms and erotically shaped
table legs are covered up with bustles and yards
of drapery. This ingenious effort might have
succeeded but for the intervention of the bosom,
which resisted all attempts at concealment and
provided Willie (or William, as he was known in
those more formal days) with sufficient
encouragement to see him through an otherwise
bad patch.

Modern Times: alimony, tights, jogging and the zipper

Increasing desperation and advanced technology have led man to develop a number of deterrents in addition to those listed above. For the most part these have failed, although the zipper has scored one or two dramatic triumphs. But it's all too late. Tempered in the crucible of battle, and more dominant than ever, the tail is now wagging the dog with a vengeance. As we shall see, its influence extends to every facet of modern life.

26

Attacks below the belt, or you can't keep a bad man down

True to his contrary nature, Willie is at his most
demanding when you already have plenty on
your mind. During those golden years between
young manhood and old age, you are at the
height of your intellectual powers and in the
midst of a brilliant career. You could stand for
Prime Minister, take over British Leyland,
discover a cure for television, open a good cheap
French restaurant – anything is possible. Or it
would be, if only your eye weren't taken off the
ball and directed elsewhere by the self-centred
little brute you take to work with you every day.

There is no escape. . . .

. . . Whatever you do, wherever you go, calamity
of one kind or another is just around the corner.

The early morning salute

Even while you sleep, the time bomb in your pyjamas is ticking. How many times have you jumped out of bed, intent on the day's business, only to look down and see that expectant form smirking up at you? You try, with some difficulty, a set of push-ups. You spend several freezing minutes under the shower. You close your eyes and think of something wholesome like sales figures.

No good. There he is, leering, perky and unbowed, ready for whatever the day will bring so long as it's trouble. How can a man apply himself to the commodities market when. vigorous attacks are being made on his concentration and his fly?

In the Underground

One of Willie's favourite hangouts, and the more
crowded it is the better. The close proximity of
all that flesh, the stimulating motion of the Tube
train, the delightful possibility of intimate
physical contact each time a bend throws
everyone off balance – this is the stuff to set the
blood coursing through the veins. And what can
you do? Bury your nose in the *Telegraph* and
hope for the best? Blame your attaché case if
challenged? Trying to move away from the
offended party is impossible. Trying to explain
makes the situation worse. Your only consolation
is that lack of room prohibits a really full-blooded
slap in the face, and nimble footwork can usually
dodge the assault on your instep from an
outraged high heel.

Would you care to come to my place tonight babe for a few drinks... this isn't really me talking... I'm under the spell of a sex-mad ventriloquist..

At the office

The trouble starts before you even reach your desk. Being unable or unwilling to distinguish between horizontal motion and vertical motion, Willie mistakes the lift for another Tube train and behaves accordingly. This time, however, it is not an anonymous member of the general public on whom he turns his attentions, but an unsuspecting girl from Claims and Adjustments on the 6th floor. As you make your escape, your newspaper held apron-fashion in front of you, giggles or scandalized whispers follow you out of the lift. Congratulations. You have just earned the title of Office Sex-Maniac, which will stand you in bad stead throughout your career.

Who invited him to the meeting?

Safe at last behind your desk, you prepare for
the first meeting of the day. Your charts are
arranged on the executive easel, your colleagues
arrive, your mind is razor-sharp, and all would
be well if it weren't for a very fine pair of legs
belonging to the Sales Promotion department
which are somewhat carelessly crossed in your
direction. The moment arrives for you to rise and
make your presentation, but of course, part of
you has already risen, making further upright
movement socially unacceptable. Your charts are
several feet away from your desk, and the only
way to reach them without giving the game
away is on all fours. Try as you might to explain
this as primal therapy it will inevitably add to
your already colourful reputation.

The business lunch

Enough has been written about lunch as a necessary tool of commerce to cover both sides of an oversized menu, but one aspect of the business lunch has so far been neglected. All learned writings on the subject assume that business lunches are conducted on a man-to-man or woman-to-woman basis, and ignore the increasingly popular trend of the bisexual business lunch. Thus you are ill-prepared when you find yourself confronted over the crudités by an attractive female executive. Be warned.

While you are engaged in hard-nosed negotiation, the third member of the party is studying the silken knees below the table, and sending urgent messages upstairs. The first sign that things are getting out of hand is a certain extravagance with the wine list, followed by an invitation to come up to your place and see your confidential computer printouts. Remorse sets in later in the afternoon, but by then the damage is done, to be commemorated next month by the arrival of your American Express bill.

Air travel

Boredom breeds mischief, and long plane trips breed boredom. This is not helped by the airlines, who all subscribe to the theory that a drunken passenger is a docile passenger, ignoring the well-known inflammatory effects of alcohol on the libido. There is, in addition, the design factor, which is guaranteed to make matters worse. For a start, it is impossible for a passenger to look a stewardess in the face unless she is bent almost double (as in the act of serving cocktails). Even then, other distractions often prevent eye contact. Not content with this, the designers have calculated the width of the aisle so that it is not quite wide enough to permit the passage of a stewardess without the aisle passenger receiving an encouraging caress on the shoulder from her thigh as she moves up and down the plane. Two or three hours of this, fuelled by whisky sours, and dinner with the client loses out to an evening of hopeful pursuit in the bar of the hotel where the airline crew is staying.

Alcohol

Say what you like about the evils of drink, but it does exert a calming influence, if taken in sufficient quantities, on your lower half. Despite his enthusiasm for a good time and a glass or two, and his belief that he can take whatever you pour down, the sad fact is that Willie has no real head for liquor. He is the life and soul of the party until called upon to do his party turn. Then, after an evening of flexing his muscles and bursting to get out and show what he can do, the moment arrives, the cage door is opened, and what do we find? The beast, curled up and dozing in the corner. Oblivious to threat or persuasion, totally unsympathetic to your feelings, he sleeps the sleep of the pure in heart, while you mutter excuses and back gracefully towards the door. The next morning, of course, he is up with the lark and looking for action while you're dealing with a terminal hangover and grave doubts about your masculinity.

Confined to bed

Medical science has been baffled for centuries by the apparent existence in the male body of two completely separate physical dispositions. Ninety per cent of you can be feeling lousy – racked with pain, twitching with fever, sore of head and red of eye – while the remaining ten per cent has never felt better in his life. Boyhood fantasies about nurses may have something to do with it, but a more likely cause is the keen competitive instinct aroused by the sight of an unsheathed thermometer. The eternal braggart, Willie can never resist showing off, and the result is that nobody takes your illness seriously, least of all the holder of the thermometer.

The social round

Invitations to parties should be treated with extreme caution, and only accepted if you have an uncontrollable social death wish. The conflict of interest is always the same: an innocent desire for relaxed conversation versus the addict's need for a fix of bad behaviour. Addiction usually triumphs, leaving behind a trail of domestic recrimination, embarrassed hostesses, vengeful husbands, alienation of affection suits, tearful phone calls, and banishment from the golf club. The penalties for attending office parties are very much the same, the only difference being that you keep your membership of the golf club but forfeit your job.

Stage fright

There are occasional periods in your life when
you and your friend are united in the pursuit of
a common dream – a vision, a soulmate, an
exquisite creature whose every prospect pleases.
Ah, love. Unfortunately, as we all know, the
course of true love never does run smooth.
Indeed, it sometimes doesn't run at all. After a
gentle succession of candlelit dinners, strolls in
the park, shared confidences and heavy florist's
bills, the time of consummation comes. Surely
the earth will move. Well, maybe it will, but not
tonight.

. . . Our Willie, suffering from an unaccustomed bout of self-restraint, is overcome by an attack of shyness and leaves you to make his apologies for him. The florist is happy to help you out.

Dancing fit to bust

For a few years now, the fashion on the dance floor has been to distance yourself from your partner as far as the crowd will allow and perform aerobic exercises. Good clean fun like this never lasts for long, and already there are signs of a growing backlash: isolated couples are not merely touching, but apparently trying to get into each other's clothes, dancing so close that wounding by belt buckle is claiming as many casualties as disco cramp. The problem here is complex. Your partner could be flattered by Willie's enthusiastic attentions, or she could summon her bouncer husband. Alternatively, she could be insulted by his lack of interest and say terrible things about you in the ladies' room. The solution is to keep a prominent bunch of keys in your trouser pocket, and these can take the credit or the blame depending on circumstances.

On the beach

A day by the seaside is likely to be a day of discomfort for both of you. Two current fashions – the almost invisible swimsuit, and jogging – combine to provide a spectacle which the Follies Bergères would be proud to have as a floor show. As the sun brings your imagination to the boil with the inevitable result, you are faced with two alternatives. The first is a crab-like dash to the water; the second is to turn over and lie face downwards. Either way, your shoulders get a painful sunburn, and your friend, whose two natural enemies are cold water and sand, sulks all the way home.

An insider's view of contraception

Few subjects have caused such lengthy disputes as this one. You, as a decent, concerned member of society, are aware of the global need for planned population. Willie, irresponsible and pleasure-seeking rogue that he is, has no thought except the thrill of the chase and the glow of conquest. Control of any kind leaves him cold, particularly when it comes in the form of what he considers an unnatural restrictive garment designed to come between him and the business at hand. With advancing age he becomes increasingly irritated by this undignified style of fancy dress and will often take evasive action. Revenge is limp.

When does hibernation set in?

Showing his characteristic perversity and poor
sense of timing, Willie retires from active service
just when you are able to give him your full
attention. Free at last from the cares of business,
nothing stands between you and the pursuit of
happiness. An experienced man of the world,
with a handsome pension and a brand new set
of dentures, the days are your own and the
nights you are happy to share. Alas, you find
yourself with a sleeping partner. He stirs from
time to time as he dreams of dimly-remembered
crimes, but he remains indifferent to the watery
gleam in your eye. You consider a transplant,
taxidermy, even Sanatogen. Finally, you take up
bridge. Life is unfair.

'A Friend Should Bear His Friend's Infirmities'

– Shakespeare

We are back in the Garden of Eden. ADAM is now an old man. He looks up as he hears a thunderclap.

VOICE FROM ON HIGH: Well, was it worth it?

ADAM strokes his beard and looks down.

WILLIE: It was more fun than having thirteen ribs, wasn't it?

ADAM says nothing.

WILLIE: We had some good times, didn't we?

ADAM nods.

WILLIE: Still pals?

ADAM: Still pals.

They shake hands.

First published 1984 by Pan Books Ltd,
Cavaye Place, London SW10 9PG
9 8 7 6 5 4 3 2
cartoons and Wicked Willie character © Gray Jolliffe 1984
text © Peter Mayle 1984
ISBN 0 330 28580 7
Printed in Spain by
Mateu Cromo Artes Graficas, SA, Madrid